STANDARD ON
Oversight Agency Responsibilities

A criterion for measuring fairness, quality, equity and accuracy

(Approved July 2010)

IAAO
INTERNATIONAL ASSOCIATION
of ASSESSING OFFICERS
Valuing the World

STANDARD ON OVERSIGHT AGENCY RESPONSIBILITIES

Revised Approved, 2020

International Association of Assessing Officers

IAAO assessment standards represent a consensus in the assessing profession and have been adopted by the Board of Directors of the International Association of Assessing Officers (IAAO). The objective of the IAAO standards is to provide a systematic means for assessing officers to improve and standardize the operation of their offices. IAAO standards are advisory in nature and the use of, or compliance with, such standards is voluntary. If any portion of these standards is found to be in conflict with national, state, or provincial laws, such laws shall govern. Ethical and/or professional requirements within the jurisdiction[1] may also take precedence over technical standards.

[1] For example, USPAP, CUSPAP, IVS, EVS.

ABOUT IAAO

The International Association of Assessing Officers, formerly the National Association of Assessing Officers, was founded for the purpose of establishing standards for assessment personnel. IAAO is a professional membership organization of government assessment officials and others interested in the administration of the property tax. Over the years IAAO members have developed assessment practice and administration standards and many of these standards have been adopted by state and international oversight agencies, and some have been incorporated into legislation.

IAAO continues at the forefront of assessment in North America and has been expanding its reach to the global community for the last five decades. Because standards form the rules by which North American assessors perform their duties, they may not be directly applicable to an overseas audience. The standards have been updated to also present the broad principles upon which the rules are based. IAAO believes those principles may be adapted to many differing statutory and regulatory scenarios worldwide.

Acknowledgments

This standard was updated in 2019 by the Standard on Oversight Agency Responsibilities Task Force chaired by T. Douglas Brydon, III. Task force members were Jennifer Rosenzweig, AAS; Julie Roisen, CAE; Robert McGee; William J. Brunelle; Darren Rasmussen, AAS; Alan Lemaster, RES; and IAAO liaison, Larry Clark. The Task Force for the Standard on Property Tax Policy, chaired by Alan Dornfest, AAS, was consulted because of the overlapping issues. The task force worked under the Research and Standards Committee, chaired by Doug Warr, AAS.

It should be acknowledged that this standard was composed in 2010, and at the time of its completion, the Technical Standards Committee comprised Joseph Hapgood, CAE, chair; Dennis Deegear; Robert Gloudermans; Bill Marchand; Mary Reavey; Nancy C. Tomberlin; and Chris Bennett, staff liaison. Special thanks to Richard Almy; Al Mobley, CAE, AAS; Wayne Llewellyn, CAE; and William Ford, AAS, for providing comments during the exposure process.

Revision notes

The 2010 standard replaced the *Standard on Administration of Monitoring and Compliance Responsibilities*, last published in July 2003.

Published by
International Association of Assessing Officers
314 W 10th St
Kansas City, Missouri 64105-1616
816-701-8100
Fax: 816-701-8149
www.iaao.org
Library of Congress Catalog Card Number: ISBN 978-0-88329-251-8

CONTENTS

1. SCOPE

This standard provides guidance on the administration of monitoring and compliance responsibilities for oversight agencies. It does not deal with the technical aspects of these responsibilities. Those aspects are covered in the published technical standards referenced throughout this document.

The need for oversight when assessment administration is decentralized has long been recognized (see Fundamentals of Tax Policy [Almy, Dornfest, and Kenyon 2008, 50– 51, 220]). Laws defining the structure of a system for ad valorem assessment usually assign responsibilities for monitoring the statutory compliance and performance of agencies conducting the primary assessment function (primary assessor) to another agency (oversight agency). In this standard the term primary assessor is used to refer to the individual assessor and/or the individual assessor's staff whom the oversight agency oversees.

This standard describes topics and issues relevant to oversight responsibilities in the United States, Canada, and other countries with similar property rights laws. A typical structure in the United States is primary assessment by cities, towns, townships, or counties with oversight by a state agency, such as a state department of revenue or tax commission. It is beyond the scope of this standard to specifically address the myriad of laws and regulations governing property rights and assessment found worldwide; however. the guidance conveyed in this standard may have relevance in any jurisdiction in which property taxes are assessed and oversight is conducted. Other IAAO technical standards, publications, and authorities should be considered and interpreted in conjunction with this standard unless expressly stated otherwise.

Local practices and jurisdictional exceptions should also be understood to align when possible.

2. PURPOSE

2.1 PURPOSE OF THIS STANDARD

The purpose of this standard is to provide guidance to oversight agencies in ensuring that primary assessors achieve uniform and equitable valuations. Effective administration by an oversight agency depends, in part, on legislation that provides clear direction and authority for the oversight agency and an appropriate budget for the necessary resources.

Actual oversight responsibilities are typically statutorily mandated. They vary widely but generally fall in the following interrelated areas:

- Setting standards and providing specifications
- Assisting and counseling primary assessors and other property tax officials
- Monitoring performance and conducting other analyses
- Enforcing laws and regulations, including equalization.

Some oversight activities relate to compliance monitoring and technical assistance for tax collection. The overall goals of oversight activities are to ensure that laws are followed, property taxes are equitable, and distributions based on equalization are fair. The activities of the oversight agency should be well-documented and transparent to all interested parties.

2.2 RESPONSIBILITIES OF OVERSIGHT AGENCIES

Governing laws set the responsibilities of oversight agencies as well as the corresponding responsibilities of primary assessors and other property tax officials. Monitoring and compliance responsibilities may include, but are not limited to, the following (in alphabetical order):

- Complex property valuation assistance/central assessment
- Education and certification of assessment professionals
- Financial assistance, cost-sharing, and budget
- Forms development
- Guidelines, manuals, and specifications
- Investigation and/or research of taxpayer complaints
- Legal and legislative responsibilities
- Performance evaluation
- Professional association involvement
- Public relations programs
- Technical research, reporting, support, and assistance.

3. COMPLEX PROPERTY VALUATION ASSISTANCE/CENTRAL ASSESSMENT

Depending on statutory requirements, oversight agencies may serve as the primary source of valuation and tax distribution for complex properties. Complex properties may be classified as, but not limited to, public utility companies (electric, pipelines, telecommunications), railroads, private railcars, airlines, and wind farms. The oversight agency should have a manual in place to define the central assessment program, which should be made available to the public. The manual at a minimum should include the following information:

- A calendar of major activities during the process and statutory deadlines
- Guidelines for the allocation of system values of each industry
- The process and methods used in developing a capitalization rate for each industry
- The methods used in determining the distribution of values and tax district information
- Models and approaches that will be considered during the valuation process including applicable cost and depreciation guides
- Exemptions available and the qualification process for those exemptions
- Penalties for erroneous or nonfiling of annual reports and instruction for filing extensions.

While the procedures and process of appraising centrally assessed companies should be completely transparent, the information provided by each company should not. Confidential information provided by these companies should be protected by the oversight agency. Annually signed confidentiality agreements between the oversight agency and each company should detail any instances in which the oversight agency may release the information provided and to whom. Any requests for the protected information not addressed in the confidentiality agreement should be denied or should be referred to legal counsel.

Other special-purpose properties, such as refineries, gas compression facilities, manufacturing plants, and the like, may or may not be handled by a primary assessor. In many instances, primary assessors contract directly with outside appraisal firms to value these special-purpose properties or seek the advice from their oversight agency. Oversight agencies may have information or manuals that can assist the primary assessor. If an oversight agency is required to contract with outside appraisal firms on behalf of the primary assessor, then those contracts should include the following information:

- Definition and scope of the appraisal
- Timelines and expected start and completion dates
- Confidentiality requirements
- Performance standards
- Contract dispute resolution
- Ownership of the appraisal
- Payment schedule.

For detailed information on contracting for assessment services, see the IAAO *Standard on Contracting for Assessment Services* (IAAO 2019). For detailed information on appeals for centrally assessed property, see Section 4 of the IAAO *Standard on Assessment Appeal* (IAAO 2016a).

4. EDUCATION AND CERTIFICATION OF ASSESSMENT PROFESSIONALS

4.1 EDUCATION

Uniform training for all assessment professionals promotes uniform application of assessment practices. Workshops, classes, and seminars should be offered by the oversight agency. Such education may be prepared in-house or by an outside agency and offered centrally or locally. If possible, fees and expenses should be defrayed by the oversight agency. Alternatively, the oversight agency should promote laws and administrative rules that encourage primary assessors to commit budgetary resources to professional education.

The oversight agency should periodically offer a well-balanced curriculum to ensure that necessary education for both new and experienced assessment professionals is available. Course catalogs should be published and provided in a timely manner so that schedules and time away from work can be arranged.

The oversight agency should keep electronic records for tracking prerequisites met and courses and workshops passed. The tracking system should be able to issue transcripts and certificates.

The oversight agency may also have a process for approval of continuing education credit for courses, workshops, and seminars offered by third parties. This provides assessment professionals with a wide variety of education options. Some oversight agencies allow web-based education to help assessment professionals in remote locations. For more detailed information, see the IAAO *Standard on Professional Development* (IAAO 2013a).

4.2 PROFESSIONAL DESIGNATION AND CERTIFICATION PROGRAMS

Oversight agencies often establish professional designation and certification programs for assessment professionals. The oversight agency should set guidelines or grant authority to another agency or board to set guidelines for implementing and administering a program. The oversight agency should establish and provide education programs supporting certification.

Certification programs can be characterized as mandatory, incentive, or voluntary. Mandatory programs require applicants to meet specified education, training, testing, and/or experience goals. Incentive programs reward successful applicants with increased pay, bonuses, or specific advancement opportunities for meeting specified goals. Voluntary programs offer applicants the opportunity to complete requirements without mandate or reward.

The three types of requirements common to oversight agency certification programs are examination, coursework, and continuing education. Some oversight agencies incorporate experience requirements as well. Individuals may be required to pass a certification examination before, or within a given period after, assuming a position. To attain or maintain their position or achieve promotions, primary assessors often must complete a variety of examinations, perhaps given in conjunction with administrators of local civil service or merit systems. Completion of coursework may be required to attain certification or achieve a position. Finally, a specified number of hours of approved continuing education within a specified period of time may be required to retain certification. Such continuing education requirements are highly desirable.

The oversight agency may offer several levels of certification to assessment professionals who complete specified coursework, examination(s), and/or experience requirements. For more detailed information, see the IAAO *Standard on Professional Development* (IAAO 2013a).

5. FINANCIAL ASSISTANCE, COST-SHARING, AND BUDGET

Oversight agencies, through the legislative process, may be responsible for providing such things as education, revaluation, computer equipment, computer-assisted mass appraisal (CAMA) systems, geographic information systems (GIS) technology, and maps. The funds provided may be distributed directly to the primary assessor, or the oversight agency may enter into agreements with vendors to provide the equipment or services to the primary assessor. In either case, the oversight agency should maintain a clear set of records showing where and how the funds are distributed and administered. Many primary assessors may be responsible for funding these items, but if any of the funding is coming from the oversight agency level, those funds should be accounted for and reviewed in conjunction with the funding from the primary assessor to ensure each project or purchase is completed.

Primary assessors who are required to finance their own education, computer hardware, and CAMA software may find it cost-prohibitive and seek cost-sharing options. Oversight agencies may find themselves in the position of organizing multiple primary assessors or participating in agreements to collectively purchase in bulk at negotiated and reduced prices, thus offering cost-saving options when compared to the once established practices.

Oversight agencies may also be responsible for the review and approval of primary assessor budgets. If so, the oversight agencies should ensure the primary assessors have adequate resources in their budget to perform their statutory duties and responsibilities. The results of performance evaluations and procedural audits may reveal areas in which a primary assessor needs to allocate funding resources. In order to promote tax equity, oversight agencies should compare budget line items, staffing levels, and overall budget between peer primary assessors. Budget review and analysis by the oversight agency may result in recommendations for budget increases, decreases, or reallocation between budget line items.

6. FORMS DEVELOPMENT

Oversight agencies should specify and, when possible, provide forms for a variety of purposes, such as assessment notices, primary assessor reports, applications for exemption, and abatement requests. Such a practice ensures uniformity among primary assessors and simplifies compilation and auditing. In instances in which electronic signatures are not legally valid, forms may be completed online and printed out for signing. Forms administered by oversight agencies should be reviewed periodically for statutory and technical changes. Oversight agencies should take responsibility for correcting, printing, and supplying (or electronically distributing) the new forms to primary assessors. Each form should follow oversight agency formatting rules and be dated with the most recent revision date to avoid confusion among different versions. When forms developed by oversight agencies are mandatory, costs for printed copies should be borne by the oversight agency. When possible, web-based applications and electronic forms should be provided, and paperless filings should be encouraged.

Oversight agencies should provide a process for primary assessors to suggest form changes. Primary assessors who develop their own forms should be required to submit them to the oversight agency for approval.

7. GUIDELINES, MANUALS, AND SPECIFICATIONS

Written guidelines, manuals, and specifications should be provided to primary assessors and maintained and updated on a regular basis. The use of written communications promotes uniform application among primary assessors.

Guidelines, manuals, and specifications should be well-written and, when practical, tested before they are provided to primary assessors. Written guidelines should always take precedence over oral communications. However, such documents do not take precedence over properly promulgated rules, regulations, statutes, and judicial decisions. For this reason, guidelines and the like should contain statements explaining limitations and proper use. An email of a document should be considered a written communication.

Guidelines should be responsive to changing market conditions. For example, changes in economic conditions can cause the market to experience large fluctuations in value. A well-planned, responsive program developed by the oversight agency with the involvement of primary assessors promotes good intergovernmental relations. Written guidelines can be an effective means of providing assistance to primary assessors in modeling, equalization, and public relations programs.

Placing guidelines, manuals, and specifications on a well-designed website allows primary assessors to obtain or consult copies when needed. Oversight agencies should communicate with primary assessors when documents are updated on the oversight agency's website.

8. INVESTIGATION AND/OR RESEARCH OF TAXPAYER COMPLAINTS

Oversight agencies may be responsible for investigating and/or researching complaints about the assessment process. These complaints would not generally be the typical disputes of valuation that are handled during the appeal process. The grievances may include disagreements as to the information collected prior to valuation, personal conflicts with the primary assessor, discrimination, incompetency, and false or erroneous information. The oversight agency should have written procedures in place to ensure that all applicable statutes are followed and that each situation is handled in a similar, fair, and equitable manner. A similar process for each complaint ensures that each is handled appropriately and in a timely manner. The guidelines should, at a minimum, ensure the following:

- Procedures are available to all parties involved in the grievance
- Documentation and resources are in place that allow a taxpayer to file a complaint with relative ease
- Complaints, notes, and any decision are communicated in writing to all parties involved
- All outcomes of the complaint or grievance are reviewed for opportunities to improve the process.

If suggestions for improvements are identified, then a follow-up investigation should be completed to confirm that those suggestions were implemented, and a written acknowledgment should be sent to all parties involved in the original grievance stating the progress of the implementation.

9. LEGAL AND LEGISLATIVE RESPONSIBILITIES

Oversight agencies should track pertinent proposed legislation. Oversight agencies should notify primary assessors of new legislation and issue bulletins explaining and clarifying legislation. When such bulletins do not suffice because of rapidly moving legislation, oversight agencies and primary assessors should develop quick-response procedures, so communication is in place at critical junctures.

Oversight agencies are often responsible for conducting research for legislative committees to determine the impact of proposed legislation and for writing the rules and regulations that implement the legislation (see the IAAO *Standard on Property Tax Policy* [IAAO 2020a]). Primary assessors should be prepared to support these functions. For studies on the impact of proposed legislation, primary assessors should serve as an information clearinghouse. Primary assessors should also participate in the process of developing rules and regulations to implement or clarify statutes. Oversight agencies should encourage such participation.

Oversight agencies should propose legislative changes when statutes limit the agency's, a primary assessor's, or a tax collector's ability to use best practices related to assessment practice, assessment standards, and tax policy.

10. PERFORMANCE EVALUATION

An oversight agency's performance evaluation of a primary assessor typically consists of multiple review and measurement aspects as directed by statutes, including the following:

- Evaluation and/or approval of the completeness and accuracy of the assessment roll submitted to the oversight agency by the primary assessor's office and as analyzed by central measures of tendency through ratio studies as defined by the IAAO *Standard on Ratios Studies* (IAAO 2013b).
- Procedural and field data quality audits
- Valuation model testing.

Evaluation and/or approval thresholds as measured through ratio studies may or may not be legislative mandates but should be considered more critical than procedural and field data quality audits. Model testing, as a function of valuation, would be required as discovered through the evaluation and accuracy of the assessment roll. Ratio studies indicate whether model coefficients require further analysis and calibration (see the IAAO *Standard on Automated Valuation Models* [IAAO 2018]).

10.1 TAX OR ASSESSMENT ROLL QUALITY AND APPROVAL

In performing an evaluation and/or approval of a tax or assessment roll, the oversight agency should perform an annual ratio study for each primary assessor. This annual ratio study should comply with the IAAO *Standard on Ratio Studies* (IAAO 2013b). This is a step toward fulfilling the primary objective of many oversight agencies to maintain equity among jurisdictions, as well as within each primary assessor's jurisdiction. The oversight agency's ratio study methods and procedures should be thoroughly documented and well-tested before application. Ratio studies should be conducted for every class of property and for as many subclasses as can be reasonably supported.

10.2 PROCEDURAL AND FIELD DATA QUALITY AUDITS

Procedural audits and field data quality audits constitute a review of operations intended to discover defective and inefficient practices. These audits should be performed to ensure that quality standards are being met. A few examples of areas that should be included in performance reviews are data collection procedures, valuation methods, and documentation of value overrides. Clear procedures should be developed so primary assessors understand what is tested and the requirements for passing, as well as the consequences and impact of failure (see the IAAO *Standard on Property Tax Policy* [IAAO 2020a] and *Standard on Data Quality* [2020b]).

10.3 VALUATION MODEL TESTING

Through ratio studies with statistical tests or, at a minimum, review of the statistical tests performed by the primary assessor, oversight agencies may determine *whether appraisal models have been calibrated properly* (see the IAAO Standard on Automated Valuation Models [IAAO 2018]).

11. PROFESSIONAL ASSOCIATION INVOLVEMENT

Oversight agencies should encourage their employees to become involved with professional associations, such as IAAO, local IAAO chapters, and local or regional assessment and appraisal associations, by participating in annual conferences, assessor working groups, educational opportunities, and committees. Greater involvement of oversight personnel occurs when membership dues and fees are paid by the oversight agency. Additional incentives for participation in professional associations can include paid conference attendance, education, and bonus rewards for earning and maintaining advanced designations.

Oversight agencies should also encourage primary assessors to become involved with professional associations, such as IAAO, local IAAO chapters, and local or regional assessment and appraisal associations. Such involvement can facilitate sharing of ideas, approaches, and best practices.

Oversight agencies should encourage primary assessors to apply IAAO standards in all assessment activities. Application of IAAO standards throughout the assessment process by the oversight agency and primary assessors promotes uniformity, equity, and professionalism.

12. PUBLIC RELATIONS PROGRAMS

12.1 PRIMARY ASSESSORS

Oversight agencies should maintain and provide an updated listing of contact personnel (names, phone numbers, and email addresses) to primary assessors. Communication programs should be established on the agency's website and through social media, email, and other communication channels. Electronic newsletters also provide a direct form of communication with primary assessors (see the IAAO *Standard on Public Relations* [IAAO 2011]).

12.2 TAXPAYERS, LEGISLATURES, AND GENERAL PUBLIC

Oversight agencies should provide brochures, press releases, slide presentations, and guest speakers to aid primary assessors with taxpayer assistance and public relations (see the IAAO *Standard on Public Relations* [IAAO 2011]). Traditional media, while still important, are beginning to be supplanted by modern social media. Interaction with users via social media should be limited and mainly informative as to deadlines and general information. Focus should be on communicating information on important dates, basic professional methodologies, local laws, and procedures as enacted for the constituency. Consistent management of the oversight agency's and the primary assessors' content and feedback is important in maintaining transparency and   professionalism.

13. TECHNICAL RESEARCH, REPORTING, SUPPORT, AND ASSISTANCE

13.1 TECHNICAL RESEARCH

Oversight agencies should maintain a research section. The section should review and evaluate valuation techniques and explore new technologies. The section should also compile, analyze, and provide general property tax and assessment-related metrics. The results should be shared with primary assessors. To the extent possible, research information should be available on the oversight agency's website. Oversight agencies should provide guidance to primary assessors of how valuation standards apply to assessment practices within the legal framework of applicable state laws. Oversight agencies should also provide research and leadership on dynamic topics affecting assessment professionals, such as natural disasters, economic challenges, and technology advancement/vulnerabilities.

Natural Disasters.

Oversight agencies should examine current laws, regulations, and guidelines for applicable direction to provide to primary assessors dealing with natural disasters like hurricanes, flooding, tornados, earthquakes, and so on. Guidance on reinspecting properties, appeals, assessment dates, and public relations should be provided. Systems to facilitate centralized collection of self-reported damage may be appropriate. Laws that are triggered when government disaster declarations are made should be considered in order to expedite reporting, assistance, relief, and recovery efforts.

Economic Challenges.

Over time, various tactical challenges to the ad valorem tax valuation legal construct may affect an oversight agency's jurisdiction. These challenges may include specialized property valuation methodologies being disputed through equalization appeals and/or the courts, proposed legislation disrupting standard ad valorem practices, rapid growth of new technologies, or unexpected large-scale economic downturns severely affecting certain classes of properties. Oversight agencies should attempt to stay ahead of such changes and provide information, guidance, and education as needed.

Technology Advancement/Vulnerabilities.

Oversight agencies may take a lead role in investigating innovative technologies that may eliminate the need for some hardware or devices, enhance data security, and improve valuation activities. For example, cloud-based services are fast becoming the norm and are a cost-effective alternative to the aging method of storing information on servers. Cloud-based services can provide for less downtime for users as hardware issues are handled in a central location rather than being in several locations with individual servers; they also allow for access outside the typical office setting because log-ins can occur anywhere. In addition, oversight agencies may provide leadership and guidance related to primary assessors' data storage practices and insurance coverage especially as they relate to protecting technology assets and data.

13.2 TECHNICAL REPORTING

Oversight agencies may be required to publish various periodic and/or annual reports summarizing performance of primary assessors, assessment statistics, equalization results, budget information, and other assessment data. These reports are typically public record and are generated for legislators, state agencies, primary assessors, and other property tax professionals. Annual and statistical reports are results of the laws and statutes that govern the oversight agency.

13.3 TECHNICAL SUPPORT AND ASSISTANCE

If permissible under statute, oversight agencies should provide technical support and direct assistance through field staff, technical publications, specialized software, and resource-sharing. Typically, a high level of service is the best way to ensure the highest level of compliance among primary assessors. Much of this service can and should be provided electronically. One specific area for which oversight agencies should provide technical support and assistance is geographic information system (GIS) mapping, which is crucial to assessment practice. Oversight agencies should be equipped to provide a CAMA system and all vital support functions to every primary assessor who cannot afford to purchase a system of its own.

Oversight agencies should support all efforts to create and maintain a common digital property base map via computer-based GIS. The property base map is the foundation of a sound, fair, and equitable property tax program. This base map has become the cornerstone of the modern surge in both governmental and private-sector productivity, an exponential growth in data creation and sharing, and massive shifts in economic landscapes.

Keeping pace with this surge has increased attention on government practices and policies. Oversight agencies should encourage collaboration and agreements with data providers and users that focus on the quality of the data, streamlining access, and reduction of costs. Authority, funding, and the establishment of standards should be a priority with the goal of avoiding a duplication of effort and data among agencies. Partnerships that forge cooperative relationships among government, the private sector, and the public should be pursued. For more information on GIS best practices, see the IAAO *Standard on Digital Cadastral Maps and Parcel Identifiers* (IAAO 2015) and the IAAO *Standard on Manual Cadastral Maps and Parcel Identifiers* (IAAO 2016b).

14. INDEPENDENT AUDIT OF OVERSIGHT AGENCY

Like primary assessors, oversight agencies can benefit from independent and objective quality assurance audits by qualified assessment professionals that have proven

- Knowledge of professional standards and the assessment profession
- Technical knowledge in areas such as property appraisal, financial, operational, management, and information technology
- Professional certification.

Typically, audits are mandated by an outside agency, and the oversight agency has no input as to who performs the review. However, if possible and practical, the review may be initiated by the oversight agency, in which case qualified assessment professionals should be involved.

In some cases, the independent audits are performed and action plans are created for the oversight agencies. The audit should be transparent, and the oversight agency should follow its direction and suggestions.

The audit may be conducted on the processes of the oversight agency. It may concern how funds are accounted for and distributed to the taxing jurisdiction. It may verify the *checks and balances* of funds within the oversight agency. In any case, the audit and oversight agency should be transparent to all clients.

REFERENCES

Almy, R., A. Dornfest, and D. Kenyon. 2008. *Fundamentals of Tax Policy*. Kansas City, MO: IAAO.

IAAO. 2011. *Standard on Public Relations.* Kansas City, MO: IAAO.

IAAO. 2013a. *Standard on Professional Development.* Kansas City, MO: IAAO.

IAAO. 2013b. *Standard on Ratio Studies. Kansas City*, MO: IAAO.

IAAO. 2015. *Standard on Digital Cadastral Maps and Parcel Identifiers.* Kansas City, MO: IAAO.

IAAO. 2016a. *Standard on Assessment Appeal. Kansas City*, MO: IAAO.

IAAO. 2016b. *Standard on Manual Cadastral Maps and Parcel Identifiers.* Kansas City, MO: IAAO.

IAAO. 2018. *Standard on Automated Valuation Models.* Kansas City, MO: IAAO.

IAAO. 2019. *Standard on Contracting for Assessment Services.* Kansas City, MO: IAAO.

IAAO. 2020a. *Standard on Property Tax Policy.* Kansas City, MO: IAAO.

IAAO. 2020b. *Standard on Data Quality.* Kansas City, MO: IAAO.

GLOSSARY

Ad Valorem—According to value.

Appeal—A process in which a property owner contests an assessment either informally or formally.

Appraisal—(1) The act of estimating the money value of property. (2) The money value of property as estimated by an appraiser. (3) Of or pertaining to appraising and related functions, for example, appraisal practice, appraisal services. Compare Assessment.

Assessment—(1) In general, the official acts of determining the amount of the tax base. (2) As applied to property taxes, the official act of discovering, listing, and appraising property, whether performed by an assessor, a board of review, or a court. (3) The value placed on property in the course of such act.

Assessment Roll— The basis on which the property tax levy is allocated among the property owners in a jurisdiction with taxing powers. The assessment roll usually lists an identifier for each taxable parcel in the jurisdiction, the name of the owner of record, the address of the parcel or the owner, the assessed value of the land, the assessed value of the improvements, applicable exemption codes, and the total assessed value. Synonyms include cadastre, list, grand list, abstract of ratables, and rendition.

Audit—A systematic investigation or appraisal of procedures or operations for the purpose of determining conformity with specifically prescribed criteria.

Central Assessment—See State-Assessed Property.

Class—A set of items defined by common characteristics. (1) In property taxation, property classes such as residential, agricultural, and industrial may be defined. (2) In assessment, building classification systems based on type of building design, quality of construction, or structural type are common. (3) In statistics, a predefined category into which data may be put for further analysis. For example, ratios may be grouped into the following classes: less than 0.500, 0.500–0.599, 0.600–0.699, and so forth.

Direct Equalization—The process of converting ratio study results into adjustment factors (trends) and changing locally determined appraised or assessed values to more nearly reflect market value or the legally required level of assessment. See Equalization and Indirect Equalization.

Equalization—The process by which an appropriate governmental body attempts to ensure that all property under its jurisdiction is assessed at the same assessment ratio or at the ratio or ratios required by law. Equalization may be undertaken at many different levels. Equalization among use classes (such as agricultural and industrial property) may be undertaken at the local level, as may equalization among properties in a school district and a transportation district; equalization among counties is usually undertaken by the state to ensure that its aid payments are distributed fairly.

Equity—(1) In assessment, the degree to which assessments bear a consistent relationship to market value. Measures include the coefficient of dispersion, coefficient of variation, and price-related differential. (2) In popular usage, a synonym for tax fairness. (3) In ownership, the net value of property after liens and other charges have been subtracted.

Independent Appraisal—An estimate of value using a model different from that used for assessment purposes. Independent appraisals are used to supplement sales in sales ratio studies or in appraisal ratio studies.

Indirect Equalization—The process of computing hypothetical values that represent the oversight agency's best estimate of taxable value, given the legally required level of assessment or market value. Indirect equalization allows proper distribution of intergovernmental transfer payments between state or provincial and local governments despite different levels of appraisal between jurisdictions or property classes. See Equalization and Direct Equalization.

Jurisdiction—(1) The right and power to interpret and apply the law; also, the power to tax and the power to govern. (2) The territorial range of authority or control.

Level of Appraisal—The common, or overall, ratio of appraised values to market values. Three concepts are usually of interest: the level required by law, the true or actual level, and the computed level, based on a ratio study.

Level of Assessment; Assessment Ratio—The common or overall ratio of assessed values to market values. Compare Level of Appraisal.*Note*: The two terms are sometimes distinguished, but there is no convention determining their meanings when they are. Three concepts are commonly of interest: what the assessment ratio is legally required to be, what the assessment ratio actually is, and what the assessment ratio seems to be, on the basis of a sample and the application of inferential statistics. When level of assessment is distinguished from assessment ratio, "level of assessment" usually means either the legal requirement or the true ratio, and "assessment ratio" usually means the true ratio or the sample statistic.

Market Value—Market value is the major focus of most real property appraisal assignments. Both economic and legal definitions of market value have been developed and refined. A current economic definition agreed upon by agencies that regulate federal financial institutions in the United States is:

The most probable price (in terms of money) which a property should bring in a competitive and open market under all conditions requisite to a fair sale, the buyer and seller each acting prudently and knowledgeably, and assuming the price is not affected by undue stimulus. Implicit in this definition is the consummation of a sale as of a specified date and the passing of title from seller to buyer under conditions whereby

- The buyer and seller are typically motivated;
- Both parties are well informed or well advised, and acting in what they consider their best interests;
- A reasonable time is allowed for exposure in the open market;
- Payment is made in terms of cash in U.S. dollars or in terms of financial arrangements comparable thereto;

The price represents the normal consideration for the property sold unaffected by special or creative financing or sales concessions granted by anyone associated with the sale.

Procedural Audit—See Audit and Procedural Edit.

Procedural Edit—An audit, or review of operations, intended to discover erroneous and inefficient practices.

Ratio Study—A study of the relationship between appraised or assessed values and market values. Indicators of market values may be either sales (sales ratio study) or independent "expert" appraisals (appraisal ratio study). Of common interest in ratio studies are the level and uniformity of the appraisals or assessments. See also Level of Appraisal and Level of Assessment.

Sales Ratio Study—A ratio study that uses sale prices as proxies of market values.

State Assessed Property—That property for which the assessed value is set by a state agency, either for taxation by the local jurisdiction affect, or for state taxation. Most often, this term applies to utility property or property with special characteristics where the state preempts local authority to achieve uniformity in assessments.

Taxpayer—(1) A person who pays a tax in the first instance, whether he or she finally bears the burden or shifts it; generally defined in law to include all persons liable for payment of a tax whether or not they actually pay it. (2) Figuratively used to mean a more or less temporary improvement that produces enough in earnings to cover taxes and perhaps some of the other carrying charges on the land. (Term should be placed in quotation marks when used in the latter sense.)

Valuation—(1) The process of estimating the value—market, investment, insured, or other properly defined value—of a specific parcel or parcels of real estate or of an item or items of personal property as of a given date. (2) The process or business of appraising, of making estimates of the value of something. The value usually required to be estimated is market value.

Value—(1) The relationship between an object desired and a potential owner; the characteristics of scarcity, utility, desirability, and transferability must be present for value to exist. (2) Value may also be described as the present worth of future benefits arising from the ownership of real or personal property. (3) The estimate sought in a valuation. (4) Any number between positive infinity and negative infinity. See Market Value.

ASSESSMENT STANDARDS OF THE INTERNATIONAL ASSOCIATION OF ASSESSING OFFICERS

Guide to Assessment Standards

Standard on Assessment Appeal

Standard on Automated Valuation Models

Standard on Contracting for Assessment Services

Standard on Data Quality

Standard on Digital Cadastral Maps and Parcel Identifiers

Standard on Manual Cadastral Maps and Parcel Identifiers

Standard on Mass Appraisal of Real Property

Standard on Oversight Agency Responsibilities

Standard on Professional Development

Standard on Property Tax Policy

Standard on Public Relations

Standard on Ratio Studies

Standard on Valuation of Personal Property

Standard on Valuation of Property Affected by Environmental Contamination

Standard on Verification and Adjustment of Sales

To download the current approved version of any of the standards listed above, visit iaao.org